Wind and Sail

Wind and Sail

A Sailing Primer

by John Muhlhausen

Chicago

Yacht Racing Magazine

Quadrangle Books

1972

Library of Congress Catalog Card Number: 79-130390
SBN 8129-0175-4

Second Printing

Book design by John Muhlhausen

In memory of Garnett Puett, a friend and fellow sailor

Preface

Within arm's reach as I write this are shelves holding dozens of "How to Sail" textbooks. Since the beginning of this century there have been dozens, perhaps hundreds more published.

So immediately one asks, "Why another?"

Basically there are two reasons for *Wind and Sail;* that is, there are two jobs to be done which we, the editors of *Yacht Racing Magazine,* feel have not been done in the dozens or hundreds of "How to Sail" texts which have preceded this one.

The first job is to isolate and simplify the *least you really have to know* to get the sails on your boat, get your boat off the beach or out of the harbor, control it to the extent that the boat goes where you want to go, and get *safely* back home again.

The second and truly unique function of *Wind and Sail* is to emphasize over and over again that *the essence of learning to sail is to know always exactly where the wind is coming from* in relation to the helmsman, and exactly the angle of your sail(s) in relation to the wind direction.

Author John Muhlhausen, whose vocation is solving difficult communications problems with creative graphics design, has achieved this latter function in a remarkably successful way, we believe. Rather than photographs of sailboats illustrating the various points of sailing, or line drawings of boats with arrows indicating wind direction, he has used color and abstract form (resulting in the kind of stylized Parcheesi board pattern you see repeated every few pages throughout most of this book).

Understand this pattern and you understand the basic lesson of sailing.

If you take Mr. Muhlhausen's cue and keep these relationships between yourself and the wind and your sails and the wind in mind all the time you're sailing, you'll be master of your sailboat.

Fail to understand and concentrate on these relationships and you'll have all kinds of unpleasant surprises out there on the water (but not dangerous ones, if you always and without exception observe the elemental rules of safety on the water).

Traditionally, "Learn to Sail" books include chapters on weather, ship's husbandry, discussions of channel markers and other aids to navigation, a colorful display of the international signal flags, chapters on how to tie knots and make decorative braids and splices, and on how to tell the difference between a yawl, ketch, schooner, cutter, sloop, and catboat. Some books will even show you how to tell the difference between a brig and a barque should there still be some square-riggers operating in your waters.

This book sticks to the real essentials. All of the above subjects (except square-rigged ships) will in time become important subjects to you. What you'll learn with *Wind and Sail* is only the beginning. There's a lifetime and more of further lore for you to absorb.

The sailboat, after all, is the most complex vehicle developed by man, with the possible exception of space ships. It operates simultaneously in air and water, and that fact, engineers tell us, introduces so many variables that by comparison an airplane or automobile is a relatively simple design problem.

When you've mastered the lessons in *Wind and Sail,* you'll feel comfortable in your boat and can begin the fascinating quest for knowledge and competence which will lead to success on either the "one-design" or "offshore" racing circuits.

Knowles Pittman
Publisher, Yacht Racing Magazine

Contents

Wind and Sail

The Lure of Sailing

Sailing means different things to different people. To some, it means stepping aboard their ocean yacht, hoisting the huge sails, and setting off on a two-week cruise. To others, it means spending a Sunday afternoon racing around a triangular course on a small inland lake, with the hope of winning a silver trophy. To still others, it means packing a lunch and taking the family out for a quiet day's sail. To those fortunate ones who have spent their entire lives sailing, it can mean an endless supply of stories to tell to wide-eyed grandchildren. At the other extreme are the envious souls on shore who watch the graceful boats glide by and wonder at the ease with which the skippers handle them. All these people have one thing in common: the lure of sailing.

Today there are hundreds of different types of sailboats of all sizes, shapes, rigs, and price ranges. When you choose a boat, it is important to consider first your ability and then your needs. The principles of sailing are the same whether you are cruising on a seventy-foot yacht or puttering around the harbor in an eight-foot dinghy. Of course, a small boat is easier to handle, easier to maintain, less costly, and consequently a better boat to learn on. So, even though a large yacht may be your ultimate dream, it is wise to start small and work up.

For purposes of demonstration, a single, simple type of boat will be considered throughout this book—a small dinghy with one mast and one sail. All complex details have been omitted.

Wind and Sail is a sailing primer. Its purpose is twofold: to educate the beginner in the basic principles of sailing, and to encourage those who have never sailed to discover the lure of wind and sail. Wholly unique is the book's use of visual images and of color to present basic principles clearly and vividly, while keeping the amount of text to a minimum.

Contrary to popular belief, there are no great mysteries to sailing, no difficult skills to master. Anyone can learn if he is willing to devote some time and effort to it. True, since it is human nature to strive for quick, easy results, many people have learned to sail without ever having read a book about it; but frequently not without boat damage or a frightening near-tragedy, both of which could have been avoided. Yet one cannot, of course, become a good sailor only by reading. Books are not a substitute for experience. All a book can do is provide the essential knowledge which every beginner must have before stepping aboard.

Before Stepping Aboard

There are three important prerequisites for the beginner before he even considers stepping into a boat. One is the ability to swim. This is absolutely necessary, not only for the obvious reason of safety, but also so that he will not be afraid of the water. Fear means lack of self-confidence, and if one is not confident of his ability, he will find it difficult, if not impossible, to become a proficient sailor. However, one should not go to the opposite extreme and develop a disrespect for the water. The sea can be very cruel at times, especially when one is under stress or strain. A healthy respect for the water is a sign of maturity.

The second important prerequisite is common sense. Know your ability and your limitations. Develop the habit of listening to the daily weather reports and learn the weather patterns of your area. If the wind is strong and small craft warnings are up, or if the skies are threatening, don't go out. Storms over water have an uncanny way of appearing suddenly, turning a placid afternoon sail into a rough experience.

When setting off for a day's sail, always anticipate the very worst and prepare for it. Chances are, nothing will ever happen, but don't take this for granted. Being prepared not only means being physically and mentally fit, but also making sure your boat is in good condition and always outfitted with the necessary safety equipment. Proper safety equipment should include: a wearable life jacket for each person aboard, a large bailing bucket which is permanently tied to the boat, an anchor, attached to an anchor line long enough for the water depth where you will be sailing, a paddle, a foghorn if you will be sailing in open waters, and such basic tools as pliers, knife, and screwdriver. Your personal equipment should include: nonskid footwear, a foul-weather jacket, and enough clothing to protect yourself from the sun. By taking these necessary precautions and using good judgment, sailing can be truly a safe and wonderful recreation. Even capsizing and falling overboard, though potentially hazardous, are certainly not as dangerous as an expressway pile-up.

The third prerequisite is to know the wind direction. Confusion about "which way the wind blows" is the biggest source of trouble for the beginner. To make it more difficult, wind direction rarely remains constant. But though variations called *wind shifts* do exist, there is always a basic wind direction which you must know before stepping aboard. There are numerous indicators, both on land and on water, which will show where the wind is coming from. The bending of trees, the path of a light falling object or of smoke, the position of a flag or weathervane—all follow the wind. Dark ripples on the water, called *cat's paws,* also move with the wind. The direction boats point when at anchor is another reliable indicator, provided they are not influenced by a strong tide or current. By far the most accurate indicator, however, is the sail. When the forward edge of it is pointing directly into the wind, the sail will flap back and forth like a flag. All these stationary indicators will show the *true wind* direction. If the boat is moving forward, the flapping of the sail will indicate the *apparent wind,* and the faster the boat moves, the more the wind direction will appear to be coming farther ahead than it actually is. The beginner must be concerned only with the true wind. Throughout **Wind and Sail,** the true wind will always be referred to as *the* wind direction.

Nomenclature

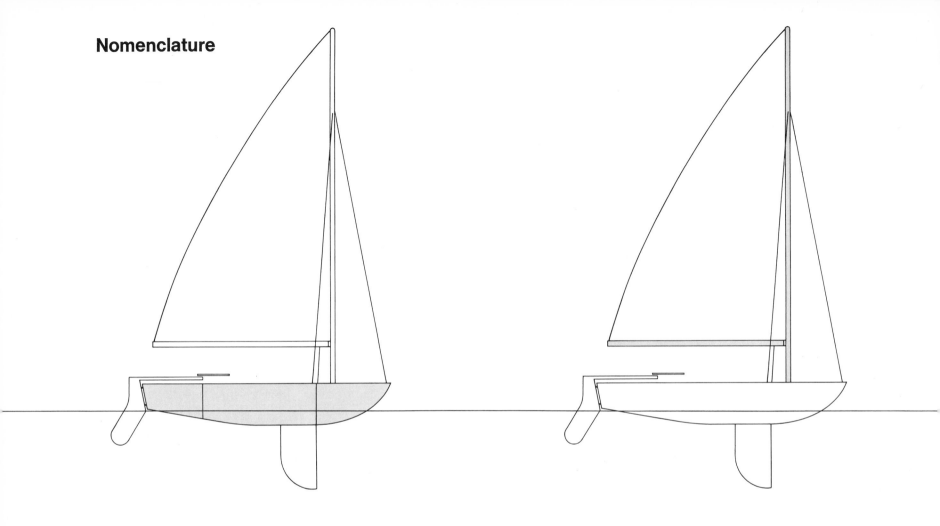

The body of the boat is the *hull*. It consists of five major parts: the front, called the *bow;* the middle, called the *midships;* the back, called the *stern;* the end surface of the stern, called the *transom;* and the top surface, called the *deck*. Some hulls have no decks and are open, while others have partial or full decks. The area inside the hull where the skipper sits is the *cockpit*. When you are sitting in the cockpit and facing toward the bow, the side of the hull on your right is the *starboard side,* and the side on your left is the *port side*. Everything in front is *ahead*, everything on the side is *abeam,* and everything behind is *aft*.

The pole rising perpendicularly from the hull is the *mast*. Attached to it is the *boom*. They are connected by the *gooseneck* fitting and are collectively called the *spars*. Supporting the mast are three wires. The two connected to the left and right sides of midships are the port and starboard *shrouds*. The wire connected to the bow is the *forestay*. Together they are called the *standing rigging*. Each shroud and forestay is individually attached to the mast by a *tang* and is in turn fastened to the hull at a *chainplate*. The length of the shrouds can be adjusted by the *turnbuckle* at the chainplate.

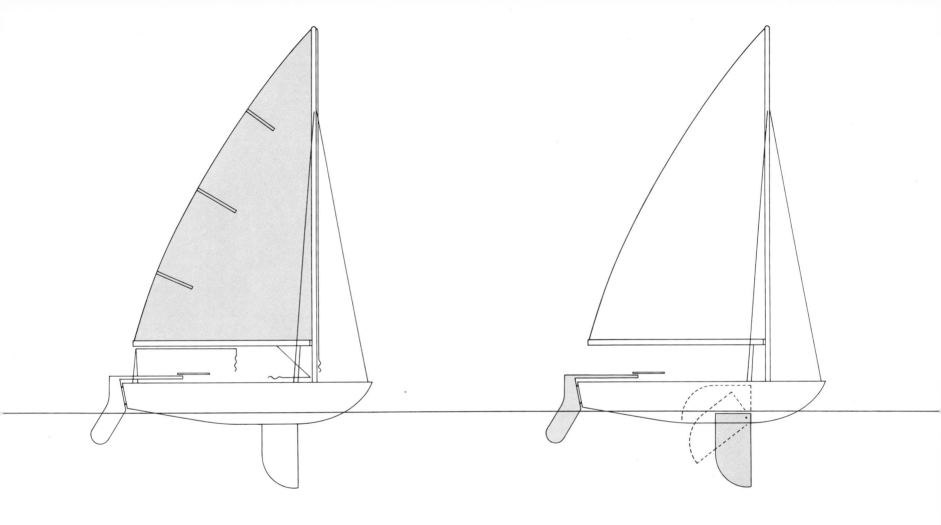

Attached between the mast and the boom is the *mainsail*. Its forward edge is the *luff*, its bottom edge is the *foot*, and its outside edge is the *leech*. Its top corner is the *head*, its inside bottom corner is the *tack*, and its outside corner is the *clew*. The mainsail is pulled up the mast by the *halyard*, pulled down by the *downhaul*, and held out by the *outhaul*. The leech is made stiff by inserting *battens* into *batten pockets* sewed into the sail. The line connected to the boom which controls the adjustment of the sail is called the *mainsheet*. The line from the boom to the lower part of the mast holding the boom horizontal is called the *boom vang*. Lines controlling the mainsail are called the *running rigging*.

The *rudder* is attached to the stern and is held in place by two pins fastened to it, which are called *pintles*. The pintles fit into two sockets mounted to the center of the transom, called *gudgeons*. The handle which attaches to the top of the rudder and extends into the cockpit is the *tiller*. Fastened to the end of the tiller is the *tiller extension*. The thin board projecting down from the center of the hull is the *centerboard*. It pivots on a pin as it is raised and lowered within the *centerboard trunk* by a line called the *centerboard pennant*. Boards which slide up and down rather than pivot are called *daggerboards*.

Rigging

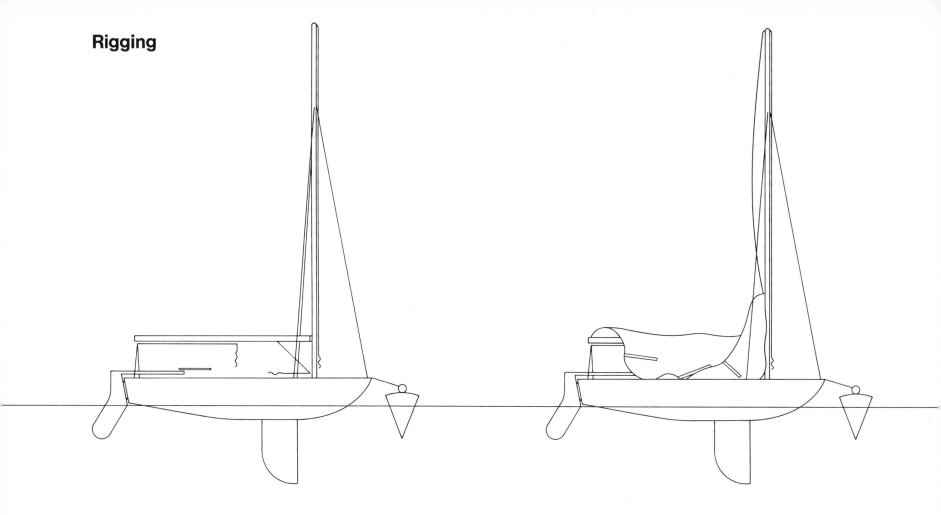

When entering the boat, always step in as close to the center of the cockpit as possible. Once aboard, lower the centerboard. See that the necessary safety equipment is aboard. Next locate the wind direction. Then fasten only the bow of the boat to the dock or mooring so that it is free to point directly into the wind. This step is most important because if it is not properly done, the boat will start sailing prematurely as soon as the sail is hoisted. Attach the rudder and tiller and make sure they and the mainsheet are completely free to move. If they are, the boat will stay pointing into the wind when the mainsail is raised.

Starting at the gooseneck, attach the foot of the mainsail by sliding it clew first along the boom. The boom and the mast either will be slotted to permit the edges of the sail to fit inside or they will have metal tracks which will accept individual slides attached to the edges of the sail. Next fasten the tack to the gooseneck and attach the outhaul, but do not pull it tight. Insert the battens, tapered end first. Before sliding the head of the mainsail onto the mast, make sure that the luff is not twisted. Undo the halyard and check to see that it is free of any obstacles, knots, or twists and attach it to the head.

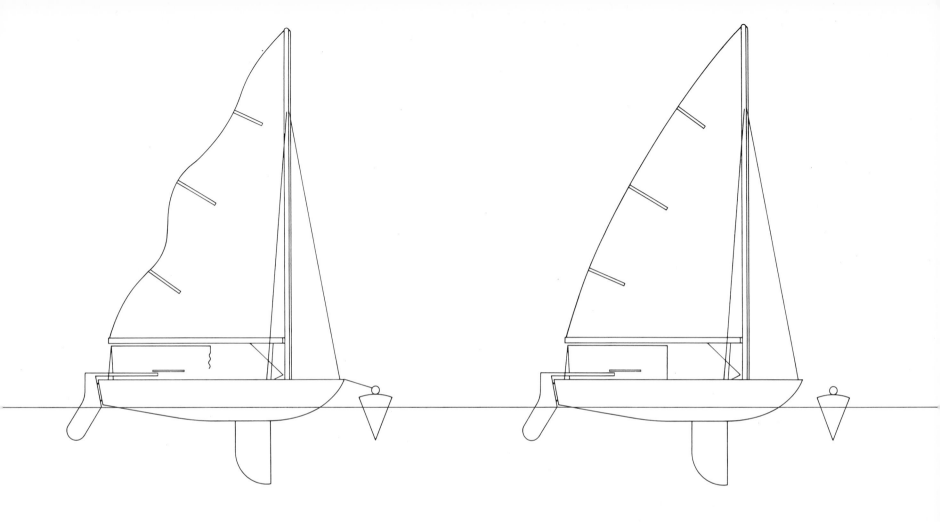

Hoist the mainsail in a slow, steady rhythm, all the time checking to see that it is not caught or twisted. Never force the mainsail. Pull it all the way up and fasten the halyard to a cleat at the base of the mast. Coil the excess halyard and stow it neatly away. The mainsail will flap. Do not try to control this flapping by pulling in the mainsheet or holding the boom, as this will immediately cause the sail to catch wind and start the boat sailing. Pull the outhaul and downhaul taut and fasten them to cleats. Finally, attach and pull the boom vang tight.

Make a final inspection to see that the rudder and tiller are properly attached and that the centerboard is completely down. Before untying the bow line, know exactly where the wind is coming from and in what direction you want to go. To cast off, untie the bow line and either push or pull the bow of the boat away from the wind, so that it heads in the direction you want to go. As the boat turns away from the wind, the sail's position will move away from the center of the boat. When the boat is headed into the desired direction, let go. To start moving, straighten the tiller and pull in the mainsheet. You're off.

Points of Sailing

In order for a sailboat to move, it must catch the wind on one side of its sail. This is done by heading the boat at various angles to the wind direction. These headings are known as *points of sailing.*

A boat heading directly into or very close to the wind direction will not be able to sail, as the wind will pass on both sides of the sail and cause it to flap. This flapping of the sail is called *luffing.* When the boat is heading in such a direction that it is possible for the sail to catch the wind, any luffing can be eliminated. However, the luffing of the sail cannot be eliminated when the boat is heading within about 45 degrees to either side of the wind direction. How close a sailboat can head to the wind varies from boat to boat. The ability of the same boat to head close to the wind will vary under different sailing conditions. To sail properly, a boat must have its sail adjusted in such a manner that if the mainsheet is let out the slightest bit, the sail will immediately start luffing along its luff edge. The position of the sail on the verge of luffing is called the *luffing point* and it determines the sail's correct angle to the wind. The relationship between the sail's angle to the wind and the boat's heading determines the *point of sailing.*

There are three major points of sailing: running, reaching, and beating. *Running* is sailing directly away from the wind with the sail all the way out at right angles to the hull. *Reaching* is sailing across the wind with the sail halfway out. *Beating* is sailing toward the wind with the sail pulled in tight. Although not considered a point of sailing and not a sailing direction, *luffing* into the wind is included here as a definite heading.

Since the sail's angle to the wind in relation to the heading of the boat determines the point of sailing, any change in heading must be compensated with a change of the sail position in order for the sail to remain on the luffing point. When the boat heads away from the wind, the mainsheet must be let out; when the boat heads toward the wind the mainsheet must be pulled in.

The movement of the boat on a point of sailing is called a *tack.* The name of the tack is determined by which side of the boat the sail is on. When the sail is on the port side, the boat is sailing on a *starboard tack.* When the sail is on the starboard side, the boat is sailing on a *port tack.* A boat sailing across the wind with the sail on the port side is referred to as reaching on the starboard tack.

Windward and *leeward* are terms used in reference to a boat's relationship to the direction of the wind. Everything closer to the wind direction is on the windward side of the boat, while everything away from the wind direction is on the leeward side. The boat's windward and leeward sides are determined by the side that the sail is on. A boat sailing on a starboard tack has its starboard as the windward side and its port as the leeward side. The general direction toward the wind is referred to as *upwind;* away from the wind is referred to as *downwind.*

In this book, color coding is used to distinguish a boat's tack and its point of sailing. Boats on a starboard tack are green, while those on a port tack are red. As the boat's heading approaches the wind direction, the red and green hues approach blue. When it heads away from the wind direction, the hues approach yellow. Pure blue or pure yellow designates either directly into or directly away from the wind, respectively. The blue arrow indicates the true wind direction.

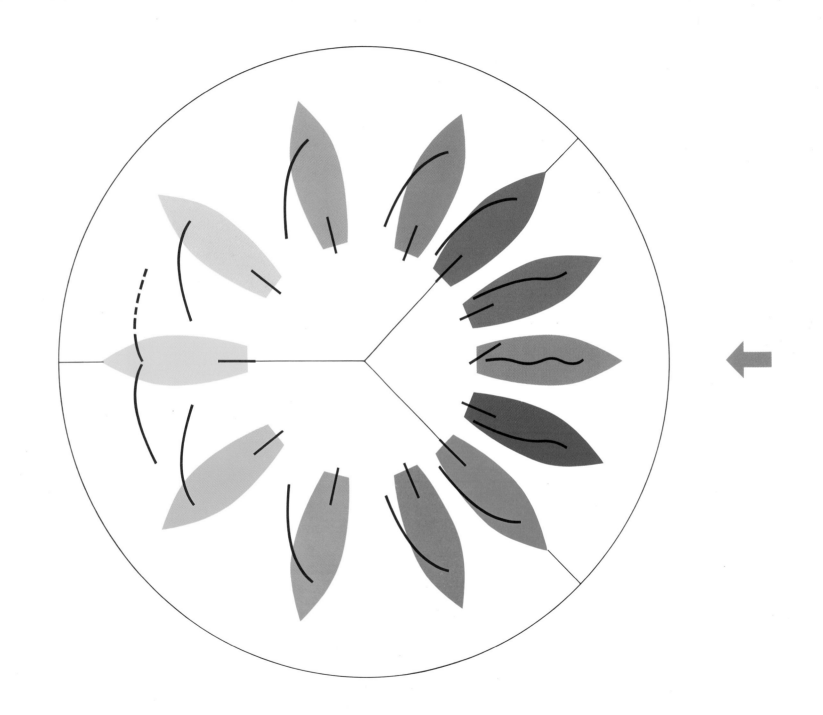

Running

Reaching

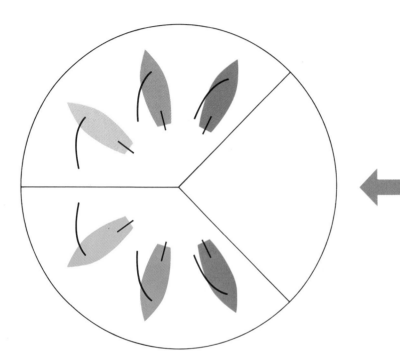

Running is sailing directly away from the wind with the sail at right angles to the hull. This is as far out as the sail can go, because the boom's forward movement is stopped by the shrouds. When sailing on a run, it is possible for the sail to function on either side although one tack is generally favored. Sailing on the tack which is not favored, called *sailing by the lee,* can cause the sail to change sides abruptly without warning. Although a run is enjoyable and easy to sail, this aspect of it can make this point of sailing a confusing and dangerous one for the beginner.

Reaching is sailing at various headings across the wind with the sail approximately halfway out. It is further defined into three minor points of sailing, each one based on a more specific heading. A *beam reach* is sailing directly across the wind with the sail exactly halfway out. In between a beam reach and a run is a *broad reach*. On this point of sailing, the wind comes more from the stern, enabling the sail to be let out farther. When the wind comes more from the bow, requiring the sail to be adjusted tighter, the boat is sailing on a *close reach*. Sailing across the wind is the fastest as well as the safest point of sailing.

Beating

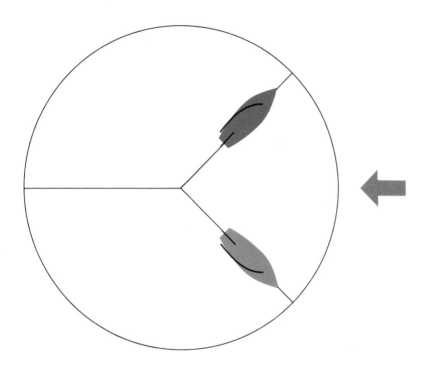

Luffing

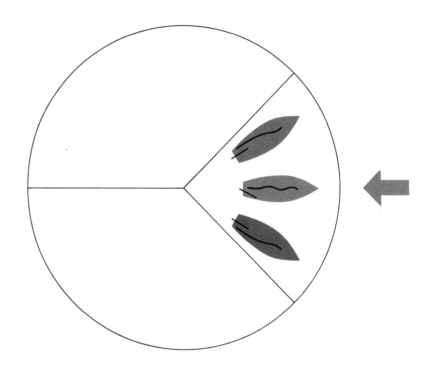

Beating is sailing with the sail pulled in tight and heading the boat as close to the wind as possible without causing the sail to luff. When sailing on the luffing point, the boat's heading is about 45 degrees to either side of the wind. Whereas a run and a reach are both determined by heading the boat either away from or across the wind and then adjusting the sail to eliminate the luff, a beat is determined by pulling in the sail tight and then adjusting the boat's heading so as to be on the luffing point. Because beating requires subtle and constant adjustment of the boat's heading, this point of sailing is the most difficult one for the beginner to learn to do well.

Luffing is not a point of sailing. It is shown to indicate that a boat will not sail effectively while heading within an area of about 45 degrees to either side of the wind. Such a close heading causes the wind to pass on both sides of the sail, making it impossible to completely eliminate the luffing. The boat will not stop sailing at the instant a part of the sail starts to luff. It will still move forward, but at a much slower rate of speed. The more the sail luffs, the more slowly the boat will move. Only when the sail is completely luffing and the boat has lost all its forward momentum will it actually come to a stop.

Maneuvers

A *maneuver* is the forward movement of the boat which causes either a change in a tack or in a point of sailing. In order to execute a maneuver, the boat must be moving, since without forward movement the rudder is useless. There are six basic maneuvers to sailing. Three require a change in tack, and three require a change in point of sailing. Coming about, jibing, and tacking all require the changing of the sail from one side of the boat to the other, while bearing off, heading up, and luffing into the wind all require an adjustment of the mainsheet and/or tiller.

To be executed properly, all these maneuvers require co-ordination between the tiller and mainsheet. This is why the skipper should handle both. This can be done quite easily in a small boat sailing in winds up to moderate strength. The skipper should always sit facing the sail in front of the tiller to enable complete freedom of movement, with the hand toward the stern operating the tiller and the hand toward the bow holding the mainsheet. This position is desirable because it gives the skipper a clear, unobstructed view ahead, puts him on the windward side of the boat for proper weight balance, and enables him to see the luff edge of the sail. Under no circumstances should the mainsheet or tiller be tied down in such a way as to prohibit the instantaneous adjustment of either.

Before any maneuver is executed it is important that the mainsheet is free of knots, that the skipper is positioned in front of the tiller and in complete control, and that there are no other obstacles in the immediate vicinity that would be adversely affected by his action. Before executing a maneuver which requires a change of tack, the skipper must inform the crew of his intentions by giving a *command of preparation* followed by a *command of execution,* at which time the maneuver is started. The other maneuvers, which require a change of a point of sailing, are not as complicated, so it is not necessary for the skipper to issue commands of preparation and execution. However, it is advisable that the skipper follow this procedure, especially while learning.

When executing a maneuver, never force the sail by pushing it into a position where it will not stay. Thanks to the wind, the sail will always go to the correct side of the boat without help. Only in extremely light air will it ever be necessary to push the sail into its proper position. Once in position, it will be necessary to adjust the sail on the luffing point.

Use of the tiller is simple, yet very critical to the proper execution of a maneuver. When the tiller is pushed to the port side, the bow of the boat will turn to the starboard. When the tiller is pushed to the starboard, the boat will turn to the port. As the tiller is pushed slowly over to one side in a steady motion, the boat will turn in a smooth arc and actually gain speed as it turns. However, if the tiller is forced over very rapidly, the rudder will go sideways to the forward movement of the boat and act as a brake slowing the boat down. When the water is rough, such action of the rudder could stop the boat and make it impossible for the skipper to complete the maneuver. The most important rule to remember while sailing is that *whenever the tiller is pushed toward the sail, the boat will always turn toward the wind; and whenever the tiller is pulled away from the sail, the boat will always head away from the wind.*

When reading about these basic maneuvers, it is important to remember not only what the maneuver is and how it relates to the wind direction but also how the various maneuvers relate to· one another. Only after the beginner establishes a firm knowledge of these maneuvers and their relationships will he be able to skillfully sail in any direction and to any destination.

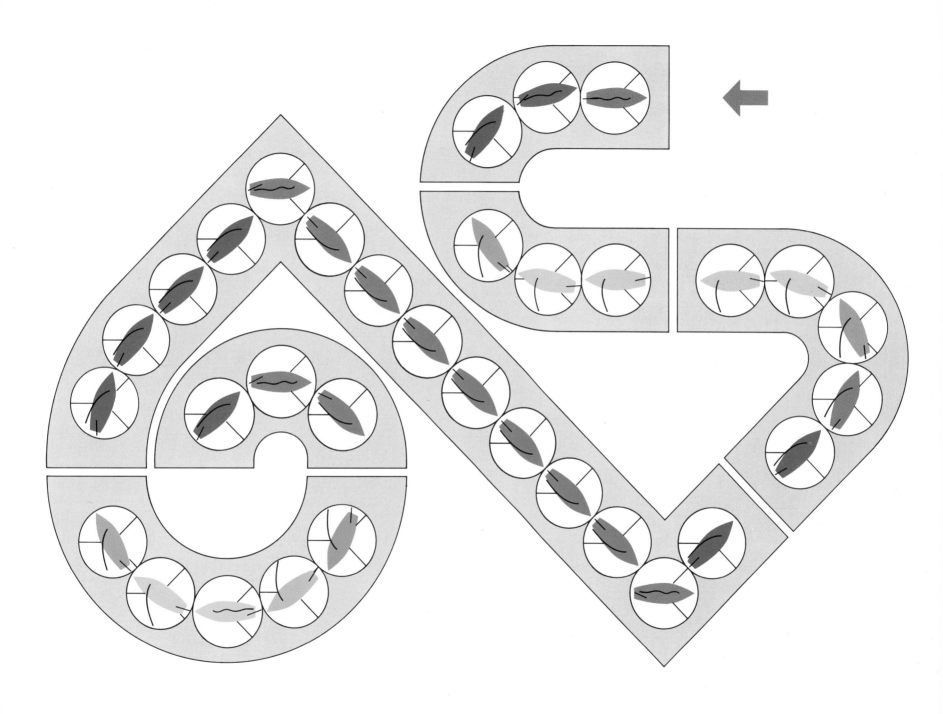

Coming About

Coming about is the turning of the bow of the boat into and through the wind direction, causing the sail to fill on the opposite side. Coming about is a safe maneuver and relatively easy to do.

Before executing the maneuver, the skipper should mentally go through his checklist and make sure the boat is moving and in proper order. The skipper then gives the command of preparation, *ready about,* which is shortly followed by the command of execution, *hardalee.* On this command the tiller is pushed to the leeward side and the boat starts turning into the wind. As the boat approaches the wind direction, it will level off and the sail will completely luff over the center of the cockpit. At this time the skipper should shift his weight to the center of the boat with his back facing the stern. As the boat continues to turn, this time away from the wind, the sail will begin to fill on the opposite side. At this instant, the skipper should let go of the tiller, switch hands on the mainsheet, and reach behind and grab the tiller with his free hand. The tiller and sail are now on the opposite sides of the boat. As the sail fills, the boat begins to lean to leeward. This is called *heeling.* When this happens, the skipper should shift enough of his weight to windward to balance the boat. At the time the sail stops luffing, the tiller is straightened. This completes the come about. The boat should now be heading on a new tack. It is important to note that during this maneuver the mainsheet is not adjusted.

As the wind velocity increases, the proper balance and correct timing become more critical because everything begins to happen more rapidly. The boat will heel more in stronger winds and will heel substantially more as the boat begins its turn toward the wind. This extra heeling is due to the boat's turning motion and will stop as the boat approaches the wind. While coming about in strong winds, the period of time when the boat is absolutely level is brief. It is during this leveling process, and when the boat begins to heel on the opposite tack, that the skipper should quickly shift his weight. If it is done too soon, the extra weight will cause the boat to heel further, and possibly to capsize; if it is done too slowly, the skipper will be caught on the leeward side as the boat heads away from the wind. This also can cause the boat to capsize. How fast the skipper should move depends on the strength of the wind and how fast the boat is turning. During strong winds it is increasingly important that the boat have sufficient forward speed to enable it to pass through the wind direction before the skipper executes this maneuver. Usually the water becomes rougher during heavy winds. This increased roughness, along with the action of the wind against the boat, will slow the boat down, causing it sometimes to get caught heading into the wind. This is called *in irons.* In irons can occur in light air as well. It can be critical when the wind is strong because it renders the boat uncontrollable. To get out of irons, the skipper must push the boom straight out to either side so that the sail catches the wind, causing the boat to sail backward. The tiller is pushed to the same side as the sail. Both the sail and the tiller are left in this position until the boat has made a backward turn pointing the bow away from the wind. The skipper can then pull in the mainsheet, straighten the tiller, and start the boat sailing forward again.

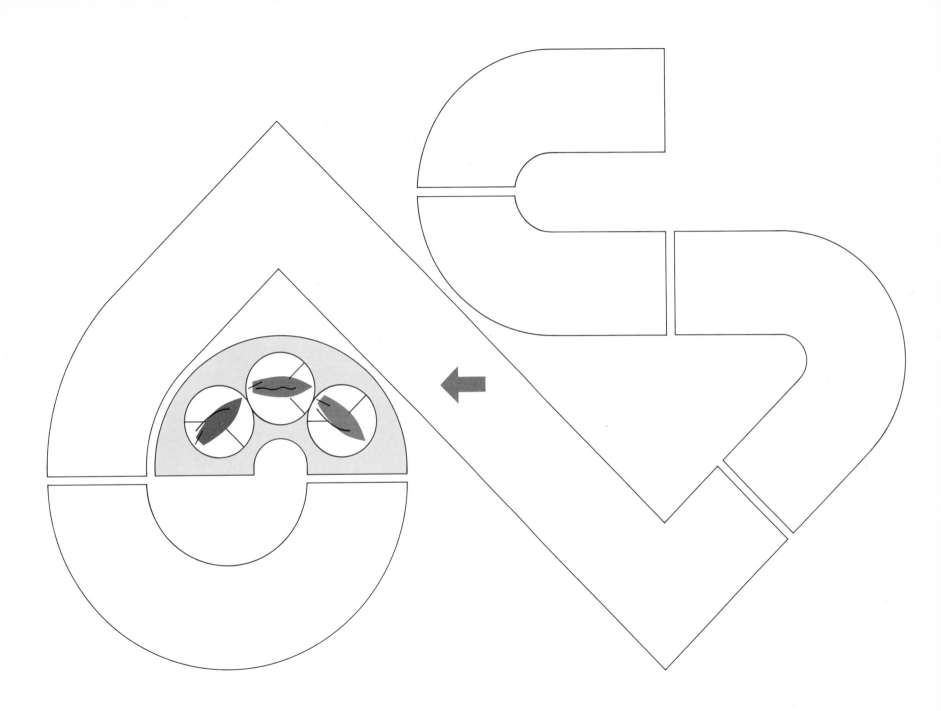

Jibing

Jibing is the turning of the stern of the boat into and through the wind direction, causing the sail to change sides. Whereas coming about requires a turn of approximately 90 degrees for completion, jibing can be done without an appreciable alteration of course. Consequently it can happen quite rapidly, and this is the hazard of jibing. Jibing is a safe maneuver if done properly, but it can be particularly dangerous if done accidentally.

During a come about, the wind causes the sail to follow the mast and to gently luff from one side of the boat to the other. During a jibe, the sail is not permitted to go forward, as its movement is stopped by the shrouds; thus the wind forces it to pass over the stern. Since the sail is not guided by the mast, but rather passes between it and the wind, the sail can go over with a great deal of speed.

The secret of a safe jibe is to control the movement of the sail with the mainsheet. This is known as a *controlled jibe.* When the jibing of the sail occurs accidentally, this is called an *uncontrolled jibe.* Usually, if the wind is light or even moderate, an uncontrolled jibe will not do any more harm than provide a good scare or a bump on the head. But in strong winds, such a jibe generally causes a capsize, and may even result in a torn sail or broken mast.

There are a number of impending signals to warn the skipper of an oncoming jibe. A jibe occurs on a run, when the boat is headed in a direction allowing the wind to come over the same side of the boat that the sail is on. When this happens, the wind begins to fill the sail from the leeward side, causing a luff which is different in appearance from the luff that occurs during a come about. This luff is a gentle puffing or soft spot in the upper part of the sail. An instant before jibing, the excessive filling of the leeward side of the sail will cause the boom to lift, applying a strain against the boom vang. If the jibe is not stopped or controlled at this point, the sail will fly uncontrolled over to the opposite side of the boat. At any time up to the moment when the sail starts to come over, the jibe can be easily and quickly avoided by gently pushing the tiller toward the sail and heading the boat closer to the wind. Before jibing, the skipper should check to see that the centerboard is down and that the mainsheet is completely clear. He should position himself in the center of the boat so he can quickly move his weight to either side when necessary. The command of preparation, *ready to jibe,* shortly followed by the command of execution, *jibe ho,* is given by the skipper. On the second command, the tiller is pulled slowly away from the sail, while the mainsheet is quickly hauled in tight so that the boom is over the center of the cockpit. Since this maneuver requires two simultaneous adjustments, it is advisable that the skipper hold the tiller under his arm, permitting both hands to be free to work the mainsheet. As the stern passes through the wind, the mainsheet is to be let out in a rapid but controlled manner so that there is no sudden snapping of sail. As the sail is being let out, the tiller is to be immediately brought back to its center position. In strong winds the boat will have a tendency to heel and continue turning toward the wind after the sail has been let out. This is called *broaching* to and is the major cause of a capsize during this maneuver. To prevent broaching it is necessary for the skipper to place his weight on the windward side and pull the tiller away from the sail so as to counterbalance the turning motion. This adjustment of the tiller should be done with restraint, as too great a turn to leeward could cause a second jibe.

By controlling a jibe in this manner, it is possible to execute the maneuver in fairly strong winds without any risks. If in doubt, it is always possible and advisable for the beginner to change tacks by coming about.

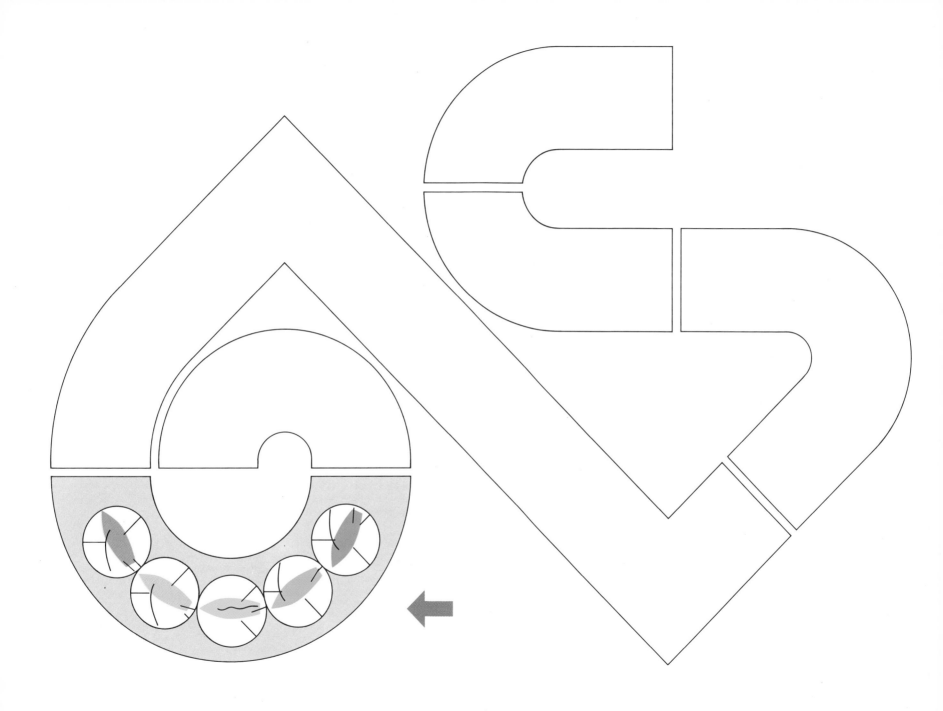

Tacking

Tacking is the process of moving the boat forward on a zigzag path by executing either a series of come abouts or a series of jibes in order to reach a desired destination. It can only be done when the boat is beating upwind or running downwind. The term tacking can also refer to one specific come about or one specific jibe. However, it is used most commonly to describe the repetition of one maneuver to achieve an objective. Sailing in a circle by coming about and then jibing would not be considered tacking.

Upwind tacking, as shown in the diagram, is beating to windward by making a series of come abouts. This is by far the most common use of the maneuver, as it is the only way a boat can sail to a windward destination that is within 45 degrees to either side of the wind. The two most difficult concepts for the beginner to comprehend while tacking upwind are that the boat cannot sail toward a destination which is directly upwind and that the boat's heading is determined by the luffing point. To properly tack upwind, the boat must be sailing on a beat with the sail in tight, heading as close to the wind as possible without the sail's luffing. This means that the tiller must be constantly adjusted to keep the sail on the luffing point, while the mainsheet remains fixed. After coming about, the skipper straightens the tiller when the sail stops luffing. This establishes the boat's new heading. In order to remain on this course, it is necessary for the skipper to periodically check the wind direction. This is done by slowly pushing the tiller toward the sail until a slight luff occurs and then pulling the tiller away just enough to eliminate it. Then the boat will always be heading as close to the wind as possible. This ability to head close to the wind is called *pointing.*

Downwind tacking is running to leeward by making a series of jibes. It is not a necessary maneuver, as is upwind tacking, since the boat can head directly for any leeward destination. The only practical use of downwind tacking for the beginner occurs when sailing in changeable winds—winds which are constantly changing in direction and or in velocity. Not running directly downwind, but rather to either side of the wind direction, greatly reduces the chances of sailing by the lee and risking an accidental jibe.

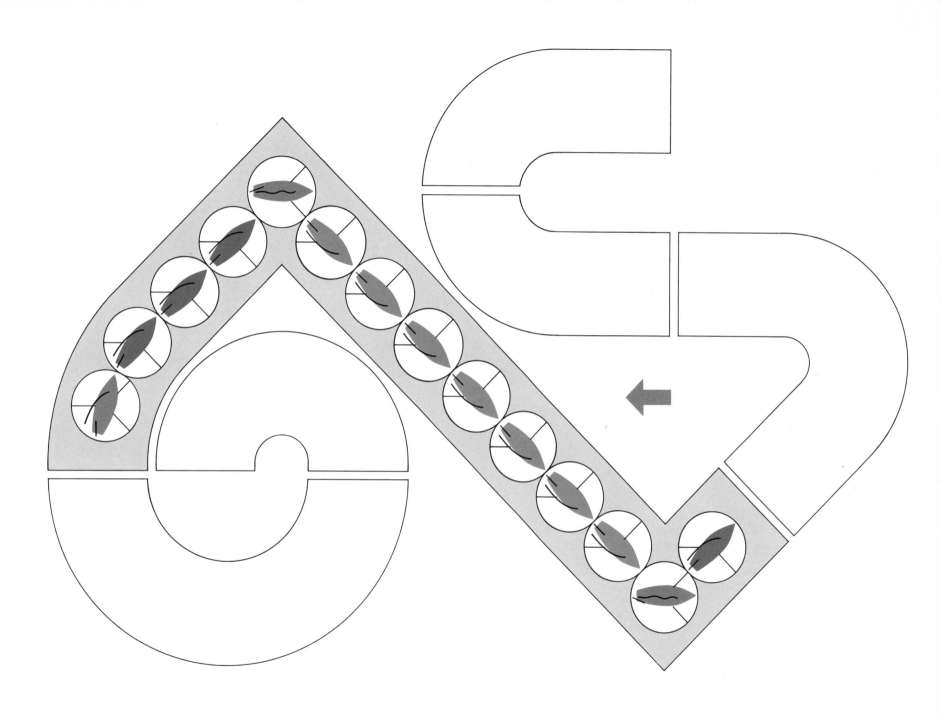

Bearing Off

Bearing off is any turning of the boat away from the wind without causing a change in tack. This maneuver always involves a change in a point of sailing.

When bearing off—i.e., going from a beat to a close reach, a beam reach to a broad reach, or a broad reach to a run—the sail must be readjusted accordingly. To bear off, the skipper slowly pulls the tiller away from the sail and at the same time slowly lets out the mainsheet. When the new heading is reached, the tiller is straightened and the mainsheet adjusted so that the sail is on the new luffing point. During strong winds, the boat will not easily bear off unless the sail is let out. This is because the sail, being too tight, presents a larger surface to the direct force of the wind and causes excessive heeling. This in turn makes the boat difficult to steer.

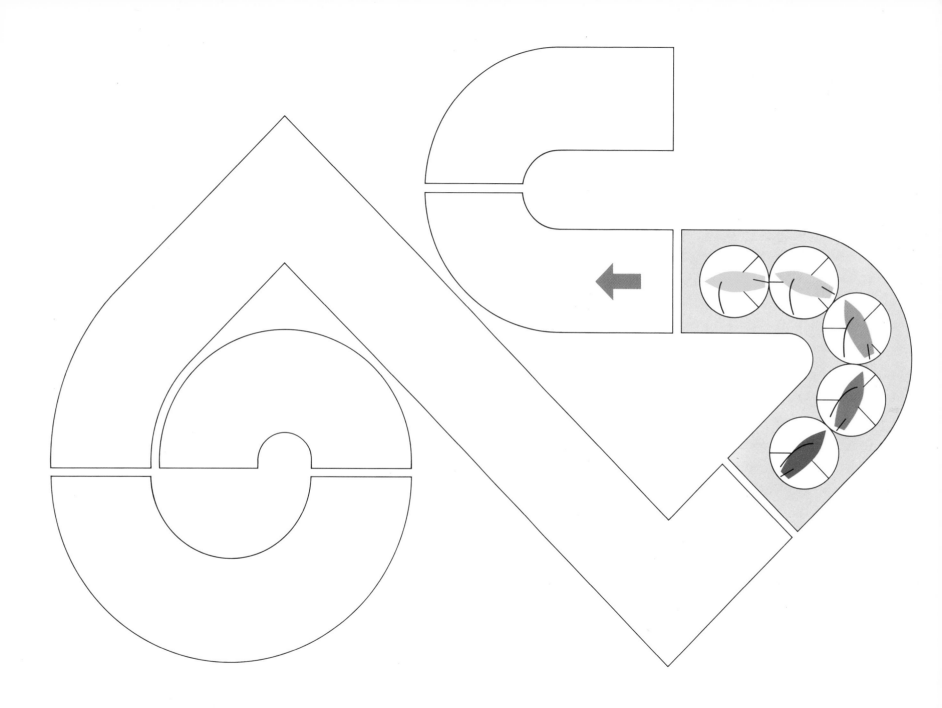

Heading Up

Heading up is the opposite of bearing off. It is any turning of the boat toward the wind without causing a change in tack or causing the boat to luff into the wind. Heading up always involves a change of a point of sailing.

When heading up from a run to a beam reach, or a beam reach to a close reach, or a close reach to a beat, the sail must be readjusted. To head up the skipper slowly pushes the tiller toward the sail and pulls in the mainsheet. When the new heading is reached, the tiller is straightened and the mainsheet is adjusted so that the sail is on the new luffing point. It is important to pull the sail in throughout the maneuver so that the boat will always maintain its forward speed.

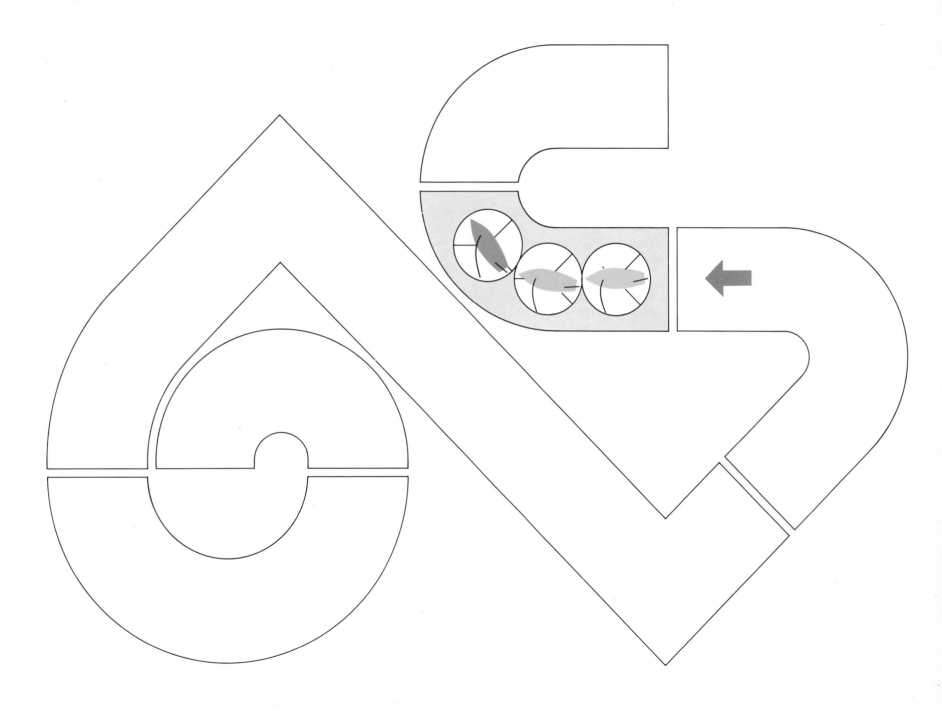

Luffing into the Wind

Luffing into the wind is the turning of the bow of the boat directly into the wind, causing the sail to luff and the boat to stop its forward movement. This maneuver can be executed from any point of sailing.

To luff into the wind, the tiller is pushed toward the sail and held there until the sail is completely luffing over the center of the cockpit. When this happens, the bow of the boat is headed directly into the wind. The skipper should then straighten the tiller and cast the mainsheet free. The boat will not stop immediately, but rather move forward at a decreasing rate of speed due to its forward momentum. While the boat is still moving, it is important that the skipper maintain his course to keep the bow from turning away from the wind. If this happens and the mainsheet is not completely loose, the boat could start sailing again. Once stopped, the boat will not stay in this position unless anchored or tied by its bow. If it is not fastened, the action of the wind and sea against the hull will cause the boat to drift backward, turning the bow away from the wind.

In light to moderate winds it is possible to stop the boat and have it remain in the general vicinity without securing the bow to some fixed object. After the boat has stopped, the tiller can be cast free. The boat will drift backward and turn at right angles to the wind with the sail all the way out and luffing. The tiller will remain on the leeward side. Only in rare circumstances should it ever be necessary to hold the tiller to leeward. The boat will drift slowly sideways, but will always remain at right angles to the wind direction. The stronger the winds, the more unstable this balance will become. Eventually the boat, if left unattended, will capsize.

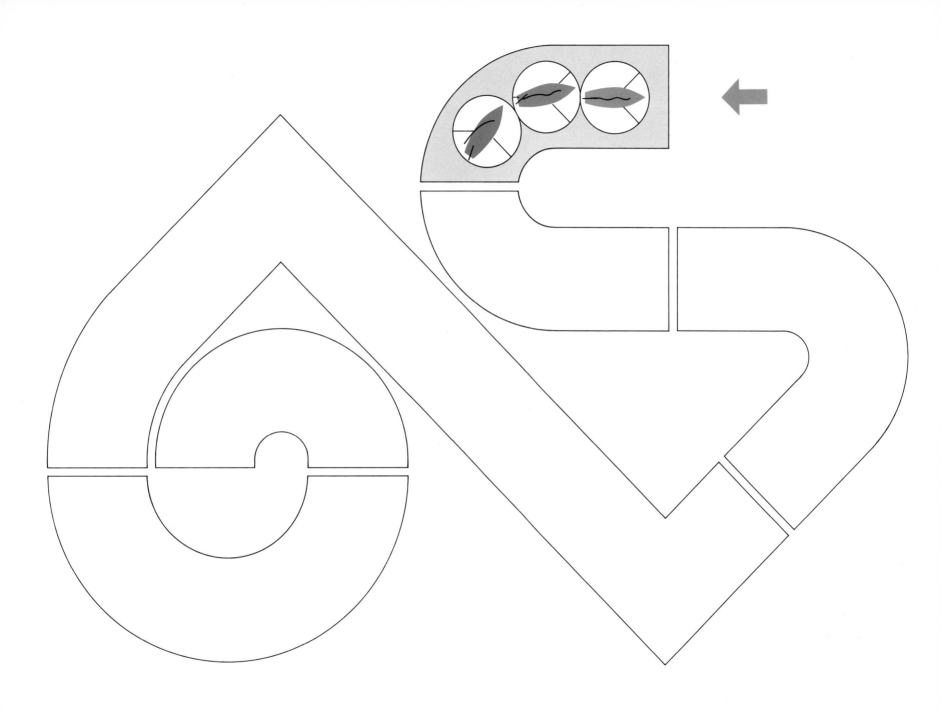

Sail Trim

Sail trim is the adjustment of the sail in order to obtain the greatest possible efficiency. In order for the sail to achieve maximum efficiency, it must first be positioned to the wind so that it is always on the luffing point. This requires a constant adjustment of either the mainsheet or the tiller. Letting the mainsheet out or heading up so that the sail luffs will cause the boat to lose power and slow down; pulling the mainsheet in or bearing off so that the luffing stops will cause it to gain power and speed up.

Proper set of the sail on the spars to obtain a smooth, evenly curved surface is also important. If the downhaul is pulled too tight, hard vertical wrinkles will form along the mast and cause the leech to fall off to leeward, ruining the even curve of the sail. If it is pulled too loose, the leech will turn to windward and hinder the free passage of air. Similar but less harmful effects will occur if the outhaul is not adjusted properly. The downhaul and outhaul should be securely fastened before casting off; however, they should not be adjusted until the skipper has had a chance to sail around and check the wind conditions. When making these adjustments, the sail should never be jerked, but rather eased into position.

Proper sail trim is also a matter of sail balance. If the sail is out of balance, this will be noticed in the balance of the tiller. Sail balance is determined by the fore and aft position of the sail area in relation to the hull's center of lateral resistance. The amount of lateral resistance is determined by the area of hull, rudder, and centerboard which is below the waterline. The center of this total area is the center of lateral resistance and is the pivot point of the boat. Too much sail area forward of this point will cause a tendency for the boat to bear off to leeward as the wind velocity increases. In order to keep the boat moving on a straight line, the tiller has to be pushed to leeward toward the sail so as to counterbalance this force. This is known as a *leeward helm* and is dangerous, because as the wind velocity increases it will be harder to head up. Conversely, if there is too much sail area behind the center of lateral resistance, the boat will have a tendency to constantly head up into the wind. To keep the boat moving in

a straight line, the tiller has to be pulled away from the sail to windward. This is known as a *weather helm.* Too much weather helm can be dangerous in high winds. If the tiller is accidentally released, the boat will come about suddenly, often not allowing the skipper enough time to release the mainsheet and change sides. In many cases this can result in a capsize. Excessive helm in either direction also has a detrimental effect on the speed of the boat through the water, as necessary tiller adjustment will cause the rudder to have excess drag. A well-balanced sail requires little adjustment of the tiller.

To correct a leeward helm, either the center of lateral resistance has to be moved forward or the sail area has to be moved aft, or in excessive cases both have to be moved. The center of lateral resistance can be moved forward by either lowering the centerboard so that it goes down as low and as far forward as possible, or by moving the skipper's weight and the position of the anchor, anchor line, life jackets, etc., as far forward as possible. As a last resort the sail's position can be moved toward the stern. This can be easily accomplished by loosening the forestay and allowing the mast to lean, or *rake,* aft. The opposite is done to correct a weather helm. Either the center of lateral resistance has to be moved aft, or the sail area has to be moved forward. Pulling up the centerboard slightly and positioning the skipper and all movable weight aft will correct most weather helms. An excessive weather helm can be corrected by tightening the forestay to pull the sail area forward.

The sail is fabricated from individual panels of material of varying widths which have been sewed together in such a manner that the sail develops a gentle curve when it catches wind. This curve or pocket of the sail is known as its *draft* and is similar in shape and function to that of an airplane wing. It is because of this shape, called an *airfoil,* that the boat is able to sail against the wind. The wind exerts pressures on the sail, which in turn exerts forces upon the hull. These forces literally squeeze the boat through the water.

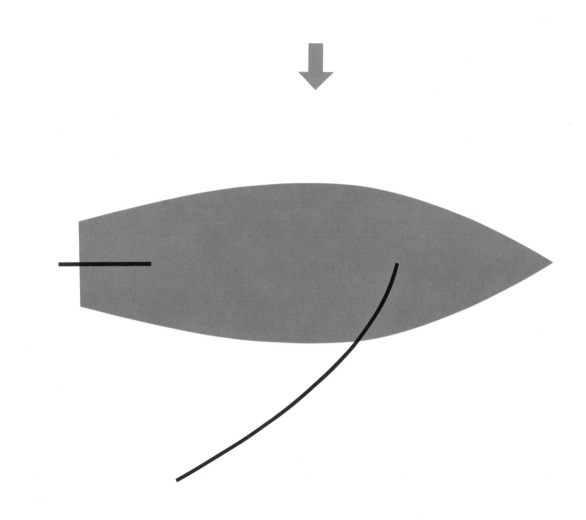

Aerodynamic Principle

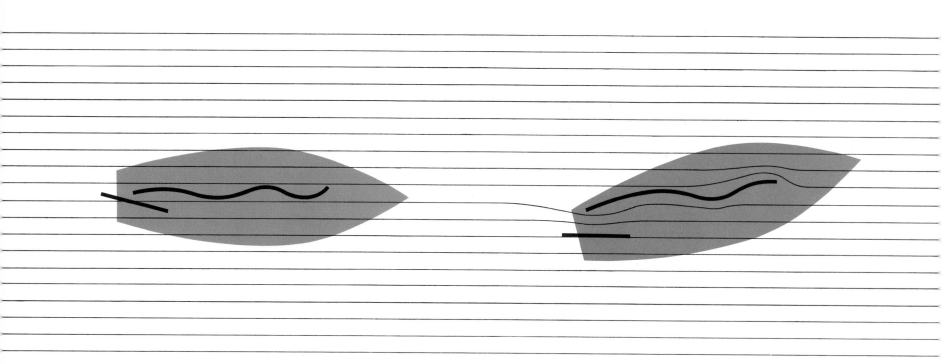

It is not difficult to understand how a boat can sail downwind. Anyone who has thrown a piece of grass into the air or cast a leaf on the water has seen how they move with the wind. But how a boat can sail upwind is not so clear. It would seem that the force of the wind against the boat would hinder any forward movement. Actually the opposite is true. Upwind sailing is based on an aerodynamic principle which is governed by the passage of wind *by* the sail rather than *against* it. This passage of air creates pressures on the sail which in turn create the boat's forward movement. The boat is actually squeezed toward the wind instead of being blown away.

The shape which the sail takes when it is full of wind is similar to an airplane wing, except that it functions vertically instead of horizontally. The moving wind is parted by the leading edge of the mast, causing it to pass on either side of the sail. The wind passing on the windward side follows, and is slowed down by, the curvature of the sail, while the wind passing on the leeward side passes freely and thus more rapidly. The faster moving air creates a low pressure along the forward leeward edge of the sail. This low pressure acts as a partial vacuum and tends to pull the sail forward, creating the boat's forward movement.

38

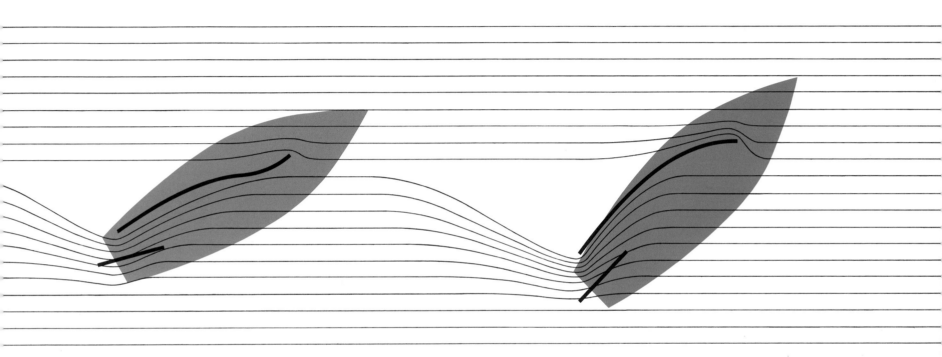

The slower moving wind on the windward side of the sail creates a higher pressure than that on the leeward side. This high pressure, as it pushes against the sail, does help to move the boat forward. However, it is largely absorbed by the stronger, more effective pulling force and contributes little to the boat's forward movement. As the boat heads away from the wind, the pushing force increases, while the pulling force decreases. When the boat approaches a beam reach, both forces are operating with equal efficiency. When the boat heads farther away from the wind, the pushing force becomes the predominant driving power. The pulling force is always present, even on a run, but its effectiveness is greatly reduced.

If the sail is improperly trimmed, the effectiveness of the airfoil becomes substantially less effective. When the boat *pinches* by heading too close to the wind, causing a luff which cannot be corrected by the mainsheet, free passage of wind by the leeward side of the sail is disturbed and the boat will slow down. When the boat *foots* by heading away from the wind with its sail in too tight, the increased angle of the sail to the wind direction hinders the wind's free escape from the windward side of the sail. If done excessively, footing will slow down the boat.

Forces upon the Hull

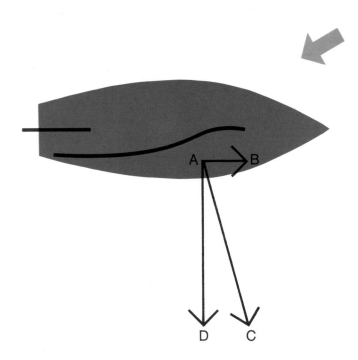

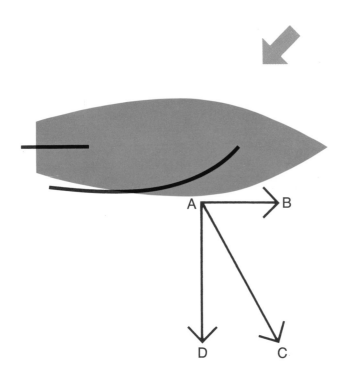

The pressure of the wind against the sail exerts two primary forces upon the hull. One is a lateral force, which is represented by the vector AD. This force presses the hull to leeward and is opposed and largely absorbed by the resistance of the centerboard to sideways movement. The other is a forward force represented by the vector AB. This force is not resisted by the centerboard and thus is free to move the boat forward. Because of this resistance, the boat squeezes forward, going in the direction of least resistance. Vector AC is the result of these two forces and represents the force of the wind on this point of sailing.

When sailing on a beat, the sail presents very little of its total surface area to the direct force of the wind; thus less energy is applied to drive the boat forward. Notice that when beating there is a considerable lateral force, as shown by vector AD. In order to reduce this force to its minimum, it is important to have the centerboard all the way down. However, when sailing close to the wind, the course steered will never be the course sailed because the centerboard does not have sufficient area to completely prevent all sideways movement.

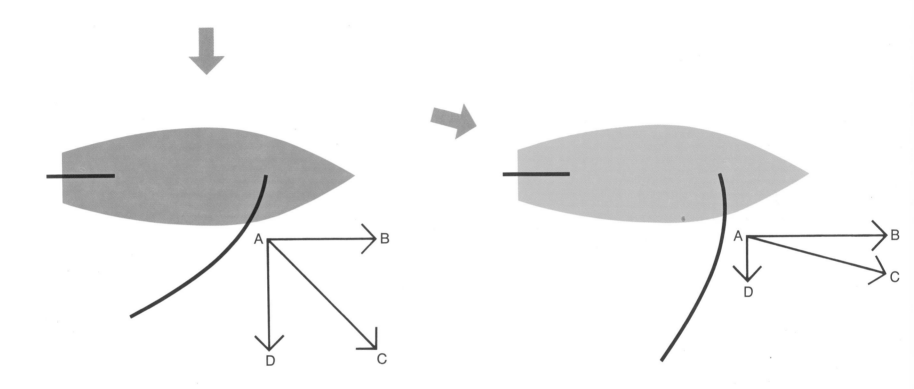

When the boat heads farther off the wind onto a reach, the lateral force lessens and the forward force increases. The need for lateral resistance is not so great as when the boat was sailing on a beat, so the centerboard can be pulled up. How far up depends upon the type of reach on which the boat is sailing. Sailing on a close reach will require more centerboard than sailing on a beam reach, and sailing on a beam reach will require more centerboard than sailing on a broad reach. When sailing across the wind, the centerboard can usually be pulled halfway up. Pulling up the centerboard reduces the area of water resistance, permitting the boat to sail faster.

As the boat approaches a run, the lateral force is reduced substantially, permitting the centerboard to be pulled all the way up. It would appear that this is the fastest point of sailing. However, this is not true, because the forward movement of the boat negates much of the wind's force. Sailing on a run also gives the skipper the false impression that the wind is blowing a great deal less strongly than it actually is. A word of caution is necessary at this point. While sailing on a run during winds of high velocity, it is unwise to pull the centerboard up completely. What the boat gains in speed it loses in stability.

Sailing Upwind

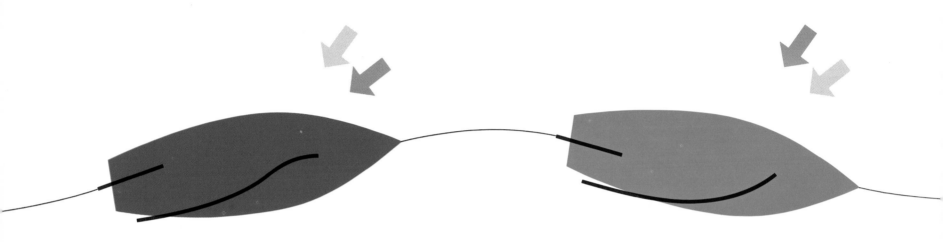

Even though it is usually possible to identify a basic wind direction, the wind rarely remains constant in its direction. Sometimes wind shifts can be quite noticeable; at other times they are slight and difficult to detect. When sailing upwind, the best way to detect a wind shift is to watch the luff of the sail. When a properly trimmed boat has been sailing on a constant course, then suddenly either the sail starts luffing or the skipper becomes aware that the sail is now in too tight; then this is due to a wind shift.

There are two types of wind shifts: a *header* and a *lift*. When the wind shifts to a new direction which is closer to the bow of the boat, causing the sail to luff, this is called a *header*. The wind has shifted in such a way that the boat must bear off from the wind in order to fill its sail. A header is similar in principle to pinching because in both cases the boat is heading too close to the current wind direction. The difference is that a header is due to a wind shift and pinching is due to the skipper's action.

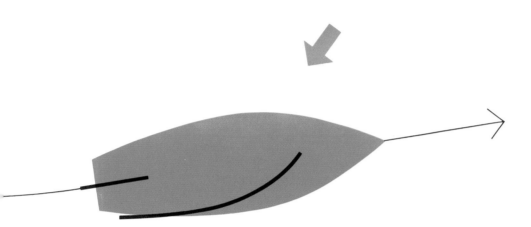

When the wind shifts into a new direction which is closer to the stern of the boat, enabling the skipper to head up without the sail luffing, this is called a *lift*. A lift is similar to footing and is not easy to identify. This is why it is important for all sailors, beginners or not, to constantly check the luffing point. The best way for the beginner to identify a wind shift is to steer the boat toward a stationary object and trim the sail accordingly. If, while sailing on this course, the boat can suddenly be steered to windward of the object, then the alteration of course is due to a lift. If the boat is not able to maintain its course toward the marker, but rather must be steered to leeward, then it is due to a header.

Sailing upwind is one of the more difficult aspects of sailing to master, because it usually involves sailing for a windward destination which usually cannot be reached on one tack. Thus it involves sailing as close to the wind direction as possible and constantly adjusting the boat's heading so as to stay on the luffing point. An experienced sailor who knows his boat can tell instantly when the sail is not properly trimmed, just by the feel of the boat's movement. This sensitivity cannot be taught; it must develop through continued careful observation of the sail and many hours of practice.

Sailing Downwind

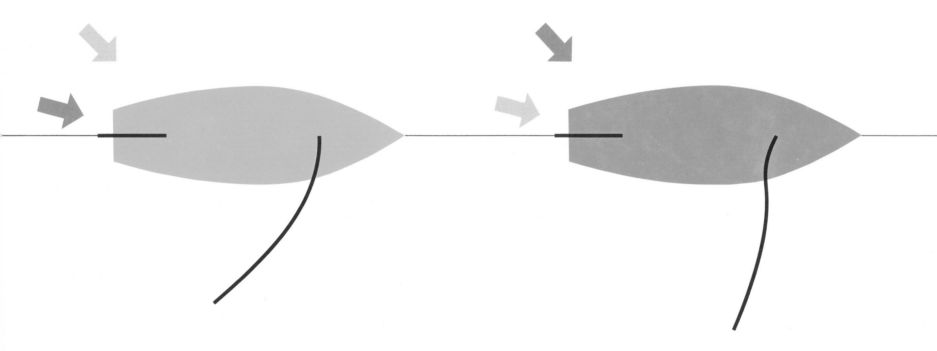

Sailing downwind is sailing on either a reach or a run. Because these points of sailing enable the boat to head directly for its destination, the mainsheet, not the tiller, is always adjusted for proper sail trim. If a header occurs while sailing on a reach, the mainsheet must be pulled in to eliminate the luff. Conversely, if a lift occurs, the sail must be let out. As in sailing upwind, a lift is difficult to notice and can often be missed.

While sailing on a run, a header will cause the sail to luff. This luffing can be easily resolved by pulling in the mainsheet. However, a lift can cause special problems. If this type of wind shift is substantial, the opposite tack could suddenly become favorable and in turn could result in an uncontrolled jibe. If this happens and it becomes apparent that the sail is about to jibe, the tiller should be slowly but firmly pushed toward the sail to offset the lift. If the shift is permanent, making it impossible for the skipper to resume his previous course, then he should jibe over to the opposite tack.

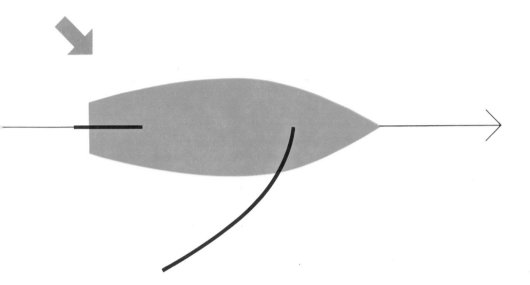

Special equipment is necessary for downwind sailing. Because wind shifts are difficult to pick up when on a run, a wind indicator is needed to identify the exact wind direction. This indicator can be a light ribbon or thread attached to the shrouds, called a *telltale,* or a pennant attached to the top of the mast, called a *masthead fly.* The other necessity is the boom vang. Its purpose is to hold the boom level so that the sail remains flat. When sailing downwind, the mainsheet does not pull the boom downward. Consequently, the force of the wind against the sail is absorbed if the boom is allowed to rise. Holding the boom level transfers the wind's energy into forward movement.

Planing is a special phenomenon which occurs usually while sailing on a beam or a broad reach. When the boat planes, it skims across the top of the water and can at times double its normal speed. The secret of planing is boat balance. When a strong puff of wind hits, the skipper should immediately hike out to windward and move his weight slightly aft so as to keep the boat absolutely level. At the same time he should pull the tiller slightly away from the boom and pull the sail in quickly. If the wind velocity is strong enough, the boat should lift up out of the water and start planing.

Capsizing

Capsizing occurs when the boat turns over on its side and cannot continue sailing until righted. During capsizing, the hull may completely fill up with water, causing the boat to swamp. When this happens, it usually means that the day's sailing is over. In the past few years, boats have been developed with a *self-rescue* or *sailaway capability*. These terms are somewhat misleading because they do not mean that this type of boat will automatically right itself and start sailing. What they do mean is that a new hull construction, along with additional built-in flotation and bailers, will enable a self-rescue boat to be righted and resume sailing. However, the effectiveness of a self-rescue hull is greatly influenced by weather, the condition of the boat, and the skill of the skipper. If the winds are strong, causing a rough sea, or if the hull has inadequate or faulty flotation, or if the skipper permits the boat to turn upside down, called *turtling,* the chances of a self-rescue are greatly reduced. Yet although this type of hull is not perfect, it does have definite advantages.

There are countless causes for capsizing, most of which can be avoided by an alert and skilled skipper. Keeping the boat upright on a windy day requires good judgment, calmness, and ability. Most capsizings are due, directly or indirectly, to excessive wind. Many apparent nonessentials—such as a carelessly executed jibe, improper boat balance, slightly damaged or inferior equipment, or an ignored wind shift, all of which can be easily overlooked in light air—become major causes of capsizes in heavy winds. A capsize can occur on any point of sailing, during any maneuver, and can happen to windward as well as to leeward. The only predictable aspect of a capsize is that it is most likely to occur uexpectedly. Thus it is important always to adhere to basic safety precautions.

If the weather is threatening don't go out. Never go out in winds which are too strong for your ability. If caught in bad weather, put on a life jacket, fasten it, and head for the nearest harbor, cove, or other protected area. Avoid sailing on a run and avoid jibing. If stranded in open water, luff into the wind, lower the sail, and anchor. If the water is too deep to anchor

in, tie the end of the anchor line to the handle of a large bailing bucket and securely fasten the other end around the mast. Then heave the bucket overboard. The open bucket will function as a *sea anchor* and will keep the bow of the boat pointed into the wind. Usually storms that come up suddenly, such as thunderstorms and line squalls, will last no longer than an hour, and it is safe to ride them out in this manner.

When the boat capsizes, there is a definite rescue procedure to follow. If the boat completely fills up and swamps, it may be necessary to lower the sail and lash it to the boom with the mainsheet before attempting to right the boat. After righting, it may be possible to bail the water out, but more likely it will be necessary to have the boat towed ashore. The rescue procedure for a boat which does not swamp and can be sailed away is similar, except for the lowering of the sail. Because of the similarity of the rescue procedures and because more and more small sailboats will be constructed for self-rescue in the future, a rescue for this type of boat is illustrated.

Having read this procedure, it is wise to go out and try capsizing. Once a skipper understands a capsize, his gain in confidence will help him to overcome any fear of heavy weather. Every sailor capsizes at least once in his lifetime; it is the grand initiation into the sport of sailing. Capsizing can be safe if the proper procedures are followed. Here is what to do:

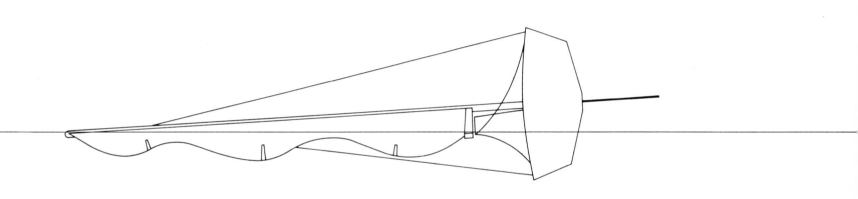

Self-rescue

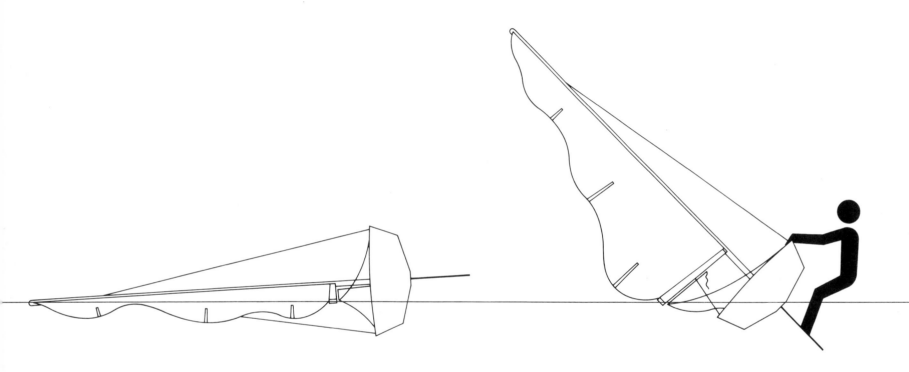

A capsizing boat usually goes over slowly, allowing the skipper enough time to climb to the high side and prepare his exit. As the boat turns onto its side, the skipper should make sure that he gets out on the high side of the boat, away from the sail, and should immediately grab the hull. This is important because a self-rescue boat will float high and can be easily blown away. Under no circumstances should the skipper ever leave the boat, no matter how good a swimmer he is. Even if the boat swamps, it will always float and thus serve as a life preserver. Besides, the hull of a capsized boat is much easier to spot than a small human head bobbing in the waves.

The righting procedure is quite simple. However, it is important for the skipper to remain calm and conserve his energy. Before righting the boat, the mainsheet should be loosened, if possible, so that the sail can run free. This is advisable because it permits the sail to luff when the boat is righted, minimizing the chance of having it capsize again. If the centerboard was up, or if it slid up after capsizing, it will be necessary to pull it all the way out into its down position. Pushing down slowly on the centerboard will enable the boat to right itself quite easily. This should be done slowly, so that the boat will not turn over onto the opposite side.

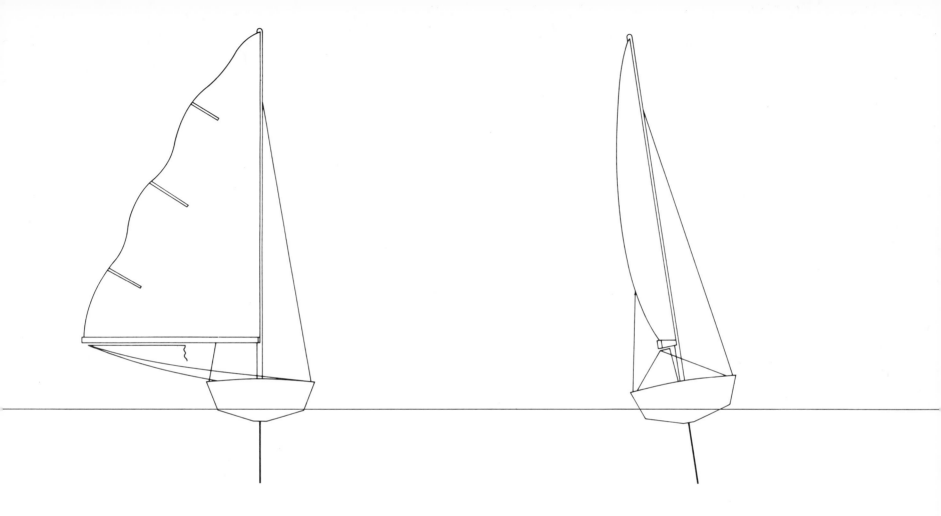

The righted boat will be relatively dry and stable enough so that the skipper can easily climb aboard. He should always climb in from the windward side to minimize the possibility of the boat's being blown or capsizing upon him. The more water in the hull, the more unstable the boat will be and the more care has to be taken when climbing aboard. Once aboard, it may be necessary for the skipper to use a bucket and bail out the major portion of the water. During this time, the sail should be allowed to luff.

Boats with self-rescue capabilities are provided with automatic bailing devices. These can be in the form of a suction-type bailer located near the bottom of the hull, just aft of the centerboard trunk, or in the form of large openings in the transom. Both types are quick and efficient bailers; however, they function only when the boat is moving. Consequently, a suction-type bailer should never be opened when the boat is idle, as water will rush back into the hull. To start the boat moving, pull in the sail slowly and straighten the tiller. Once the boat is underway, the bailers can be opened.

Rescue for Turtling

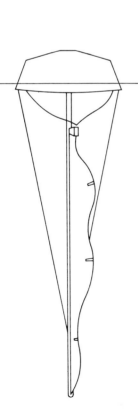

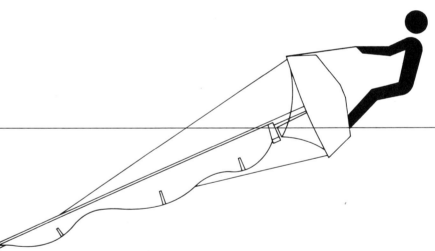

The rescue of a boat that has turned *turtle* is difficult. Not only is this position extremely stable, but also the centerboard has most likely dropped back into the centerboard trunk, making it hard to apply any effective leverage. The best method is for the skipper to secure the mainsheet to a cleat within the cockpit and run the end of the mainsheet over the top of the hull. By standing up and leaning back while applying pressure with his feet against the bottom of the hull, he can usually pull the boat up to its side position. From here on the foregoing rescue procedure can be followed.

Towing

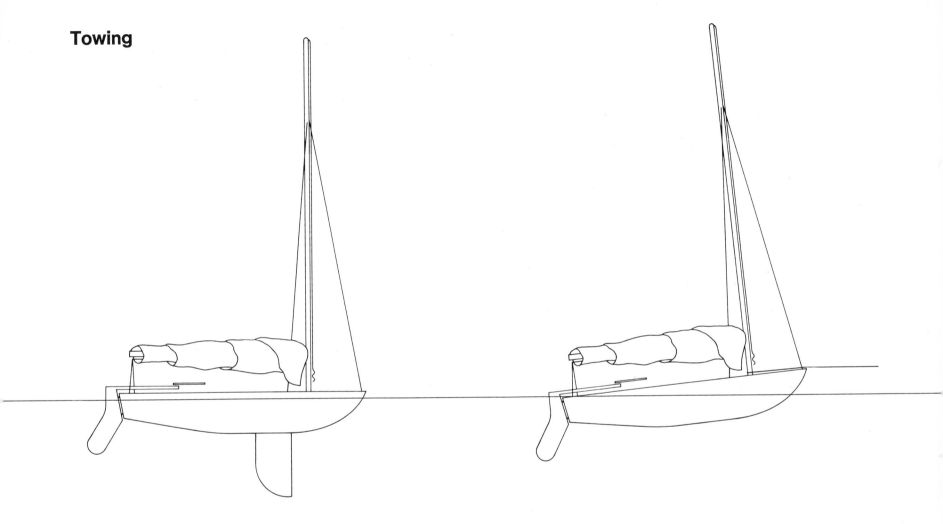

To be safely towed, the boat must be upright. If the boat is swamped, it will be necessary to lower the sail and wrap it around the boom. The anchor line can be used for towing. The skipper should untie the anchor and fasten that end of the line around the lower part of the mast. He should then lead the line toward the bow forward of the shrouds, to the towboat. Next the centerboard must be pulled up. Before being towed, the skipper should move his weight as far aft as possible to lift the bow out of the water. Although water may come in over the stern, this is not serious and will stop as soon as the boat starts moving.

A small boat full of water can weigh a ton or more. Because of its fragile construction, any sudden strain can cause damage. Thus it is important that the towboat start slowly and maintain a moderate, steady speed throughout the tow. The boat being towed must be steered directly behind the towboat. Since a swamped boat is extremely unstable, any course steered to either side can cause it to capsize. Once it is moving, however, the bailers can be opened.

Landing

It is natural for a beginner to feel apprehensive about landing, especially if the harbor or dock is crowded. And even experienced sailors will worry when landing in unfamiliar areas, thinking of possible damage to their own and other boats. Much of the beginner's apprehension is based on fear of not being able to shut off the force of the wind, since he knows that a sailboat does not have brakes or an engine to put into reverse. Actually this is only partially true. By skillful use of the wind and the sail, he can spill the force of the wind, apply the brakes, and even make the boat sail in reverse.

The initial approach for a landing can be made from any direction or on any point of sailing. However, the final approach must always be made from leeward, with the boat headed directly toward the wind. Only by allowing the sail to luff will it be possible to spill the force of the wind. Because of its forward momentum, the boat will not stop the instant the sail starts luffing. Thus it is important that the final approach start far enough to leeward to provide sufficient distance for losing momentum. Forward momentum, caused by the weight of the boat and the speed at which it is traveling, will vary between boats and sailing conditions. Under identical sailing conditions, heavier boats will develop more momentum than lighter boats and after turning into the wind will coast farther and be more difficult to stop. The faster a boat moves, the more momentum it will develop. However, identical boats traveling at identical speeds will not coast as far in rough seas as they will in calm water. The variables are numerous. When beginning or when sailing a new or unfamiliar boat, it is best to allow more distance for the final approach than necessary. It is far better to fall short and try again, or paddle the remaining distance, than risk the chance of damage.

Usually a landing can be made easily by just luffing the sail and coasting upwind to the mooring or dock. However, in some cases it is necessary to stop the boat as quickly as possible. This is done by backwinding the sail. The force of the wind against the back side of the sail will function as a brake and quickly stop all forward momentum. If backwinding is continued after the boat has stopped, the boat will eventually begin to sail backward. There will be times when lack of sufficient space to leeward makes it unwise to attempt a landing under sail. Under such circumstances it is best to luff up nearby, lower the sail, and paddle to the mooring or dock.

Conditions for landing are always changing, and the ability to execute a good landing under these various conditions is acquired through constant practice. It is best to learn in open water where there will be enough room to try different approaches toward something small which cannot be easily damaged or cause damage to the boat. An extra life cushion or life jacket is a good marker for this type of practice, since it does not have to be anchored. Even though it may be constantly moving, it will help the beginner develop the necessary skill for a real landing.

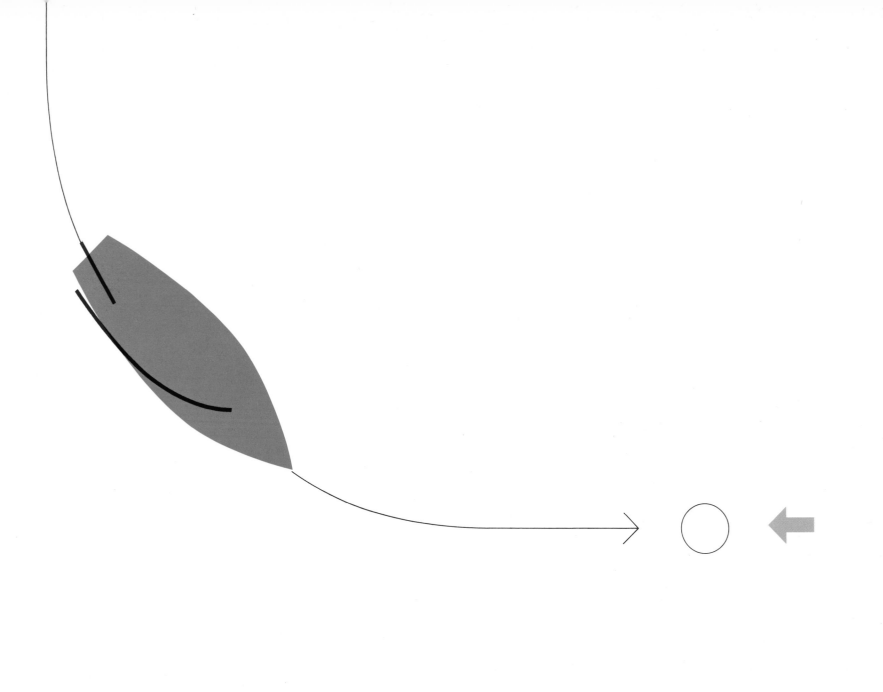

Fetching a Mooring

Landing at a Dock

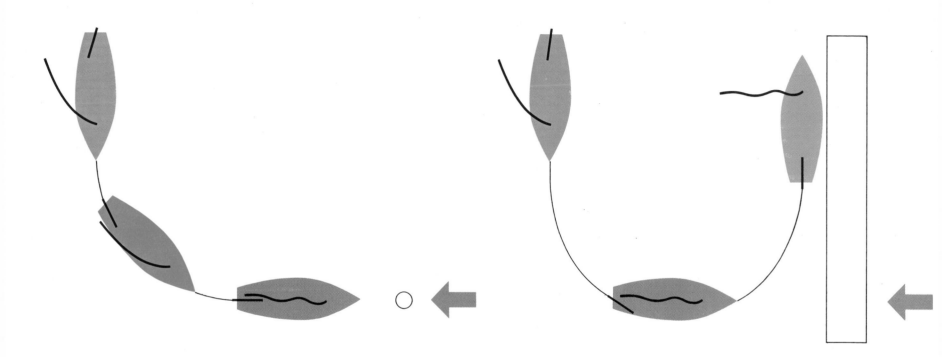

When directly downwind, the skipper should luff into the wind, loosen the mainsheet, and steer for the mooring. Upon reaching it, he should turn slightly so that the bow passes to the leeward side. At this time he can release the tiller, go forward, and pull the mooring line aboard. The line must be led in front of the shroud and immediately fastened. Once the boat is securely attached, the sail can be lowered. Picking up the mooring line while the boat is still moving will usually stop its momentum; however, if the boat is going too fast, it may cause it to pivot around to the windward side of the mooring and cause complications.

The final approach is the same, but the distance required to lose forward momentum has to be estimated more carefully. Whereas a mooring is a small, movable object that can easily be passed, a dock is a large, fixed obstruction which is hard to avoid. Thus it is important, when executing this landing, to come in slowly. If the approach falls short, the skipper can usually heave a line to someone on the dock and be pulled in. If not, he has the option of either trying again or of paddling in. When there are no boats nearby, he can coast alongside the dock to lose additional forward speed and minimize the risk of an accident.

Rescuing a Man Overboard

Backwinding

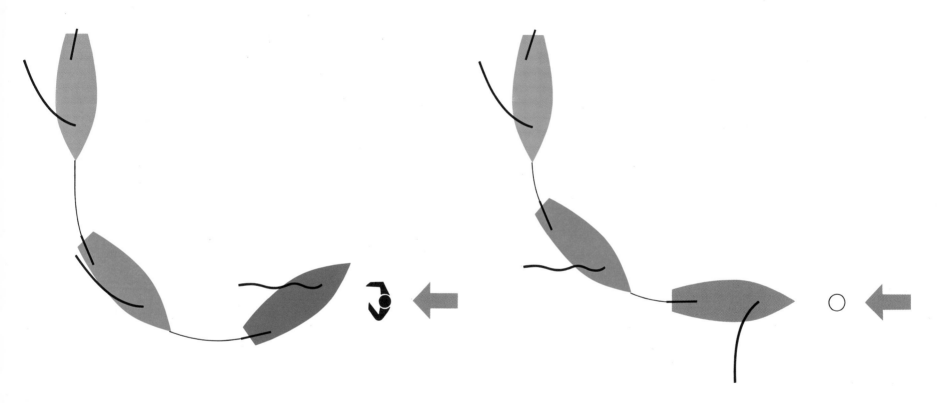

Again the approach is the same. This time, however, it is extremely important to fall slightly short. Unlike a mooring or a dock, a man overboard is not stationary and is probably being pushed toward the boat. If the person is conscious, the skipper should stop the boat several yards to leeward and toss him a life jacket which has been attached to a long line. Then the person can be easily pulled toward the boat. If he is unconscious, it will be necessary to bring the boat to him. The skipper should never leave the boat. Regardless of the rescue, the person should be brought aboard over the windward side.

Backwinding is an emergency procedure which can be used to slow down the boat on its final approach. On a small boat this can easily be done by grabbing the boom and pushing it out to either side, forcing the sail against the wind. The pressure of the wind will create an immediate backward thrust which will gently offset the boat's forward momentum and bring it to a complete stop. If backwinding is continued, the boat will eventually begin to move backward.

The Language of Sailing

Abeam   At right angles to the side of the boat

Adrift   A boat floating free, loose from the mooring

Aft   Toward the stern

Aground   Touching the bottom of a body of water

Ahead   In front of the bow

Airfoil   The shape the sail takes when it is hoisted and drawing

Apparent wind   The wind direction shown by a moving wind indicator

Astern   To the rear; behind

Backwinding   The pushing or pulling of the sail against the wind

Battens   Wood or plastic strips that stiffen the leech of the sail

Batten pocket   Sewn enclosure in the leech of the sail which holds the batten in place

Bear off   To turn away from the wind

Beat   To sail close to the wind, closehauled

Bend   To fasten a line; to put the sail on the spars

Boom   Spar that supports the bottom edge of the sail

Boom vang   Line that holds the boom level when sailing on a reach or run

Bow   The forward part of the hull

Bowline   Mooring line attached to the bow; painter

Broach to   The turning of a boat broadside to the waves or wind

Bunk   The bed on a boat; sleeping quarters

Capsize   To turn over on the side

Cat's paws   Small ripples on the water caused by the wind

Centerboard   Thin board or metal plate that functions as a retractable keel on a small sailboat; fits into the centerboard trunk

Centerboard pennant   Line that controls the vertical position of the centerboard

Centerboard trunk   The enclosure for the centerboard

Chainplate   Fitting on the boat to which the shroud or forestay attaches

Clew   Lower aft corner of the sail

Cockpit   Open space within the hull for skipper and crew

Come about   To turn the bow of the boat into and through the wind direction, causing the sail to change sides

Command of execution   A warning given by the skipper when starting a maneuver

Command of preparation   A warning given by the skipper before starting a maneuver

Daggerboard   A centerboard that moves vertically

Deck   Top surface of the hull

Downwind   Away from the wind, to leeward

Downwind tacking   Running to leeward by making a series of jibes

Draft   The pocket of the sail

Fetch   To reach a desired destination

Foot   Bottom edge of the sail; to sail with sail adjusted too tight

Forestay   Stay that runs from the bow to the upper part of the mast

Forward   Toward the bow

Galley   A yacht's kitchen

Gooseneck   Fitting that attaches the boom to the mast

Gudgeon   Fitting that attaches to the transom and holds the rudder in position

Halyard   Line that hoists the sail

Haul   To pull

Head   Top corner of the sail; the boat's toilet

Header   A wind shift toward the bow

Head up   To turn toward the wind

Heel   The leaning of the boat

Helm   The tiller, or the wheel on larger yachts

Hull   The body of the boat

In irons   Caught heading into the wind, unable to complete tacking

Jib   A small, triangular-shaped sail used at the bow

Jibe   To turn the stern of the boat into and through the wind direction, causing the sail to change sides

Leech   Aft edge of the sail

Leeward   Away from the wind, downwind

Leeward helm Improper boat balance that causes the bow of the boat to bear off to leeward

Lift Wind shift toward the stern

Line Working rope

Luff Forward edge of the sail; flapping of the sail; also, to turn the boat into the wind

Luffing point The instant the sail starts to luff

Mainsail Primary sail

Mainsheet Line that adjusts the position of the mainsail

Marry To tie two lines together

Mast Spar that supports the front edge of the sail

Masthead Top of the mast

Masthead fly A wind indicator located at the masthead

Midships Middle part of the hull

Mooring Fixed anchorage for a boat

Outhaul Line that pulls the sail out on the boom

Pinching Sailing too close to the wind

Pintle Fitting that attaches to the rudder and fits into the gudgeon

Planing When the wind lifts the hull on top of the water and causes the boat to increase its speed

Point To sail closer to the wind

Points of sailing Headings at various angles to the wind direction

Port Left side of the boat when looking forward

Port tack Sailing with the sail on the starboard side

Rake The fore or aft leaning of the mast

Reach To sail across the wind

Rudder A thin board which attaches to the transom in line with the centerboard and controls the boat's direction

Run To sail away from the wind, before the wind

Running rigging Lines which are constantly being adjusted

Sailing by the lee Sailing more than 180 degrees away from the wind

Sail trim The adjustment of the sail to obtain the greatest efficiency

Sea anchor A bucket or other drag used to slow the boat or head it into the wind

Self-rescue *(sailaway)* A boat that under proper conditions is able to be righted and continue sailing

Shipshape Everything in its proper place

Shrouds Stays which run from the side of the boat to the top of the mast

Spars Supports for the sail, mast, and boom

Standing rigging Fixed lines or cables

Starboard Right side of the boat when looking forward

Starboard tack Sailing with the sail on the port side

Stern The aft part of the hull

Stern line Mooring line attached to the stern of the boat

Stow To put away in its proper place

Tack The lower forward corner of the sail; movement of the boat on a point of sailing

Tacking To bring the boat about or jibe; a series of come abouts or jibes

Tang Fitting on the mast to which the shroud or forestay attaches

Telltale A wind indicator attached to the shroud

Tiller The handle used to steer the boat

Tiller extension An extra handle which is attached to the inboard end of the tiller

Transom The end surface of the stern

True wind The wind direction shown by a stationary wind indicator

Turnbuckle Fitting that adjusts the length of the shroud

Turtle A capsized boat that has turned upside down

Upwind Toward the wind, to windward

Upwind tacking Beating to windward by making a series of come abouts

Weather helm Improper boat balance that causes the bow of the boat to head up to windward

Windward Toward the wind, upwind

Index

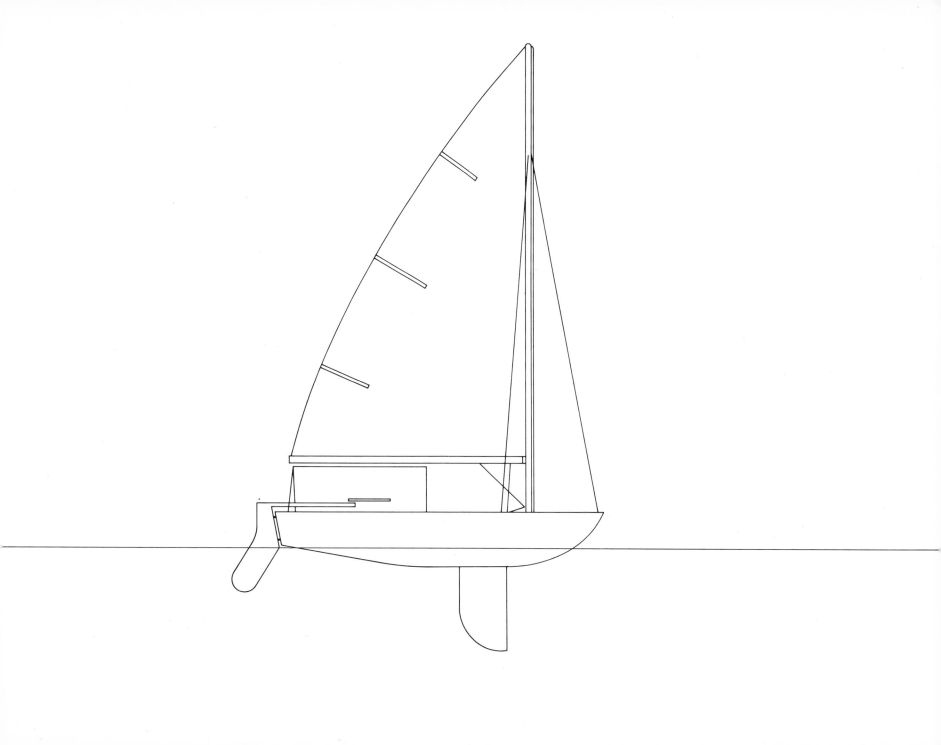